To:

_____

From:

_____

Date:

_____

40 Days

of

Jesus
Always

Joy in His Presence

Sarah Young

THOMAS NELSON
Since 1798

Published in Nashville, Tennessee, by Thomas Nelson. Thomas Nelson is a
registered trademark of HarperCollins Christian Publishing, Inc.

Unless otherwise noted, Scripture quotations are taken from the Holy Bible,
New International Version®, NIV®. Copyright © 1973, 1978, 1984, 2011 by
Biblica, Inc.® Used by permission of Zondervan. All rights reserved worldwide.
www.Zondervan.com. The "NIV" and "New International Version" are
trademarks registered in the United States Patent and Trademark Office by
Biblica, Inc.®

Scripture quotations marked KJV are from the King James Version. Public
domain.

Scripture quotations marked NASB are from New American Standard Bible®.
Copyright © 1960, 1962, 1963, 1968, 1971, 1972, 1973, 1975, 1977, 1995 by The
Lockman Foundation. Used by permission. (www.Lockman.org)

Scripture quotations marked NKJV are from the New King James Version®. ©
1982 by Thomas Nelson. Used by permission. All rights reserved.

Any Internet addresses, phone numbers, or company or product information
printed in this book are offered as a resource and are not intended in any way
to be or to imply an endorsement by Thomas Nelson, nor does Thomas Nelson
vouch for the existence, content, or services of these sites, phone numbers,
companies, or products beyond the life of this book.

Library of Congress Cataloging-in-Publication Data

ISBN 978-1-4002-2172-1

Printed in the United States

20 21 22 23 24   POL   5 4 3 2 1

Introduction

Dear Reader,

I believe the message of joy is extremely important at this time—for people throughout the US and around the world. With joy-filled reminders from the Word of God, may the pages of this book invite you into a new way of living by embracing a life of joy.

The devotions in this book are written from the perspective of Jesus speaking to you, the reader. I have included Scripture with each devotion, and I encourage you to read both—slowly and prayerfully. Let us be assured that God is in control and He is good.

I will be praying for readers of *40 Days with Jesus Always*. For any of you who do not yet know Jesus as Savior, I'll be asking God to bring you into His family of believers.

Remember that Jesus is with you at all times. May you experience His presence and His joy in ever-increasing measure.

Sarah Young

IN ME YOU CAN DISCOVER *Joy inexpressible and full of Glory*! You will not find this kind of pleasure anywhere else; it is available only in your relationship with Me. So trust Me, beloved, and walk confidently along your life-path. As we journey together, you will encounter many obstacles—some of which are quite painful. Expect these difficulties each day, and don't let them throw you off course. Refuse to let adversity keep you from enjoying Me. In My Presence deep sorrow can coexist with even deeper Joy.

Your life with Me is an adventure, and there are always some dangers involved in adventurous journeys. Ask Me to give you courage so that you can face your troubles boldly. Keep your hope fully fastened on Me and on the heavenly reward that awaits you. Your Joy will expand astronomically—beyond anything you could possibly imagine—when you reach your eternal home. There you will see Me *face to Face*, and your Joy will know no bounds!

1 PETER 1:8 NKJV; 2 CORINTHIANS 6:10;
1 CORINTHIANS 13:12

ALL THINGS ARE POSSIBLE WITH ME! Let these powerful words light up your mind and encourage your heart. Refuse to be intimidated by the way things look at the moment. I am training you to *live by faith, not by sight*.

The sense of sight is a spectacular gift from Me, to be used joyfully and gratefully. However, it's easy to be mesmerized by all the visual stimulation surrounding you—and forget about Me. Faith is a type of vision that connects you to Me. Instead of being so focused on the visible world, *dare* to trust in Me and My promises.

Live close to Me, your Savior and Friend, but remember: I am also infinite God. When I lived on your planet, *My miraculous signs revealed My Glory, and My disciples put their faith in Me.* I continue to do miracles in your world, according to My will and purposes. Seek to align your will with Mine and to see things from My perspective. Exert your faith to ask for big things, and *watch in hope for Me* to work.

MARK 10:27 ESV; 2 CORINTHIANS 5:7;
JOHN 2:11; MICAH 7:7

7

I AM WORTHY of *all* your confidence, *all* your trust. There are people and things that deserve *some* of your confidence and trust, but only *I* deserve all of it. In a world that seems increasingly unsafe and unpredictable, I am the Rock that provides a firm foundation for your life. More than that, I am *your* Rock in whom you can *take refuge*—for I am *your God.*

You must not let your circumstances define your sense of security. Though it is natural for you to want to be in control of your life, I can empower you to live supernaturally, resting in My sovereign control. I am *a well-proved help in trouble,* and I am always present with you. I help you face unwelcome changes, and even catastrophic circumstances, without fear.

Instead of letting anxious thoughts roam freely in your mind, lasso them by voicing your hope in Me. Then bring those captive thoughts into My Presence, where I will disarm them. *Whoever trusts in Me is kept safe.*

PSALM 18:2; PSALM 46:1–2 AMP;
2 CORINTHIANS 10:5; PROVERBS 29:25

THE JOY I GIVE YOU transcends your circumstances. This means that no matter what is happening in your life, it is possible to be joyful in Me. The prophet Habakkuk listed a series of dire circumstances that he was anticipating, then he proclaimed: *"Yet I will rejoice in the Lord, I will be joyful in God my Savior."* This is transcendent Joy!

I am training you to view your life from a heavenly perspective—through eyes of faith. When things don't go as you had hoped, talk with Me. *Seek My Face* and My guidance. I will help you discern whether you need to work to change the situation or simply accept it. Either way, you can teach yourself to say: "I can still rejoice in *You*, Jesus." This short statement of faith—expressing your confidence in Me—will change your perspective dramatically. As you practice doing this more and more, your Joy will increase. This training also prepares you to handle the difficulties awaiting you on your pathway toward heaven. *Rejoice in Me always.*

HABAKKUK 3:17–18; PSALM 105:4 NASB;
PHILIPPIANS 4:4

BE JOYFUL ALWAYS; pray continually. The way to rejoice at all times is to find moment-by-moment pleasure in your relationship with Me—the Lover of your soul. This relationship is so full of comfort and encouragement that it's possible to *be joyful in hope* even when you're in the midst of adversity.

Give thanks in all circumstances. There is immense Power in praying, "Thank You, Jesus." These three words are appropriate for all times and in every situation because of My great sacrifice for you. I encourage you to praise Me for every good thing as soon as you become aware of it. This practice adds sparkle to your blessings—heightening your Joy.

When you are feeling sad or discouraged, it is still a good time to thank Me. This demonstrates your trust in Me and brightens your perspective. To enhance your gratefulness, ponder specific things about *Me* that delight you—My continual Presence, My lavish grace, *My unfailing Love.* Thanking Me in all circumstances strengthens your relationship with Me and helps you live more joyfully!

1 THESSALONIANS 5:16–18; ROMANS 12:12;
EPHESIANS 1:7–8; PSALM 143:8

BLESSED ARE ALL THOSE WHO WAIT FOR ME!
Waiting patiently does not come easily to you, but it is
nonetheless very good for you. You long to plan ahead,
make definitive decisions, and make things *happen*.
There is a time for that, but this is not the time. Now
is a time for sitting in My Presence, trusting Me with
your whole being. This discipline will bring a wealth
of blessings your way.

Some of the good things I offer you reside in
the future. While you obediently wait on me, you
are building up equity for those not-yet blessings.
Because they are veiled in the mystery of the future,
you cannot see them clearly. Other blessings are for
the present. The very process of waiting for Me is bene-
ficial. It keeps your soul on tiptoe, as you look up to
Me in hope. You acknowledge that I am in control,
and you rest in My goodness. Though you may not
understand why you have to wait so long, I bless you
as you choose to *trust Me with all your heart.*

ISAIAH 30:18; PSALM 143:8 NKJV;
PROVERBS 3:5 ESV

THROUGH MY RESURRECTION from the dead, you have *new birth into a living hope*. My work in you is all about "newness." Because you belong to Me, you're *a new creation; the old has gone, the new has come!* Your adoption into My royal family occurred instantaneously, at the moment you first trusted Me as Savior. At that instant, your spiritual status changed from death to life—eternal Life. You have *an inheritance that can never perish, spoil, or fade—kept in heaven for you.*

You are indeed a new creation, with the Holy Spirit living in you. But your becoming a Christian was only the *beginning* of the work I'm doing in you. You need *to be made new in the attitude of your mind and to put on the new self*—becoming increasingly godly, righteous, and holy. This is a lifelong endeavor, and it is preparing you for heaven's Glory. So receive this assignment with courage and gratitude. Be alert, and look for all the wonderful things I am doing in your life.

1 PETER 1:3–4; 2 CORINTHIANS 5:17;
EPHESIANS 4:22–24; ROMANS 6:4 NKJV

ALWAYS BE PREPARED to give an answer to everyone who asks you the reason for the hope you have. It is easier to obey this command when you're well rested and your life is flowing smoothly. It's quite another matter when you're feeling exhausted and frazzled. Yet *this* may be the time when your hopeful answer will make the greatest impact. So make it your goal to be prepared *always.* You also need to be ready to answer *everyone* who asks you the reason for your hopefulness. It is tempting to judge some people as poor candidates for learning about Me and what I mean to you. But only *I* know their hearts and the plans I have for them.

Essential preparation for giving a good answer is living in awareness of My Presence—trusting Me fully as your Hope. This will steady you as you deal with the frequent ups and downs of your life. Whenever you're struggling, encourage yourself by pondering truths of the gospel and by gazing at Me, your glorious Hope.

1 PETER 3:15;
ROMANS 5:5 NASB; PSALM 27:4

YOU CAN TRUST THE ONE who died for you. In this world of spin and scams, people often find it hard to believe anyone. They talk about requiring others to "earn" their trust by proving themselves. *I* am the quintessential Person who has earned the right to be trusted. For your sake, I left the glorious perfection of heaven and began life in your world as a helpless, stable-born infant. I resisted all temptations for thirty-three years so that My sacrifice for sinners would be sufficient. I lived a perfect life and freely gave My body to be tortured and executed—to pay the full penalty for sin. As a result of My death and resurrection, *whoever believes in Me has eternal Life*!

I want you to rely confidently on Me—not only as your Savior but also as the God-Friend who is taking care of you. I have already proved how trustworthy I am. Now I invite you to relax in My loving Presence and confide in Me. Tell Me your hopes and fears. *Cast all your anxiety on Me because I care for you.*

2 CORINTHIANS 8:9 NKJV;
JOHN 3:36; 1 PETER 5:7

THANK ME FOR THE GLORIOUS GIFT of forgiveness. I am your Savior-God, and I alone can give you this blessing. I went to exorbitant expense to procure this gift for you. You receive forgiveness and become My child by receiving *Me* and *believing in My Name.* This Name, Jesus, means *the Lord saves.* To receive this gift of salvation, you need to trust Me as your only Hope—the One who delivers you from all your sins.

There is no condemnation for those who are in Me. I want you to enjoy the wonder of walking through your life as My follower—totally forgiven! The best response to this wondrous gift is to live in gratitude, seeking to please Me above all else. You don't need to do good things to secure My Love, because it's already yours. Just let your desire to please Me flow readily out of your grateful heart. Thanking Me frequently will help you stay close to Me, ready to follow wherever I lead. Rejoice, beloved, for *through Me the law of the Spirit of Life has set you free!*

JOHN 1:12; ACTS 4:12 NASB;
ROMANS 8:1–2

As you SEEK ME, I encourage you to *rejoice and be glad in Me.* Take time to praise Me in psalms and song. Think about who I am: I dwell in *splendor, majesty, and beauty.* Then remember how I left the Glory of heaven and came into the world—so I could bring you into My kingdom of everlasting Life and Light. All of this helps you to *be joyful in Me, your Savior.* This Joy ushers you further into My holy Presence, helping you draw nearer to Me. And this nearness gives you even more reason to rejoice!

Being joyful blesses not only you but other people. Your family and friends will benefit from your gladness, which can rub off on them. You can also influence many beyond your inner circle. When My followers are joyful, unbelievers are more likely to be drawn to Me. Joy shines in stark contrast to your ever-darkening world, and some people will ask you about it. *Always be prepared to give an answer to everyone who asks you the reason for your hope.*

PSALM 70:4; PSALM 96:6 ESV;
HABAKKUK 3:18; 1 PETER 3:15

MY KINGDOM IS NOT OF THIS WORLD; it is indestructible and eternal. When you see shocking evil and mismanagement all around you, do not despair. As I was being arrested, I told My disciples that *I could call on My Father and He would send more than twelve legions of angels* to rescue Me. However, this was not the plan We had chosen. It was necessary for Me to be crucified—to save *everyone who calls on My Name*.

Remember that you are part of My kingdom of everlasting Life and Light. The darker your planet becomes, the more you need to cling to the hope you have in Me. Despite the way things look, I am in control, and I'm accomplishing My purposes in ways you cannot understand. Though this world is deeply fallen, it's possible to live in it with Joy and Peace in your heart. As I told My disciples, so I say to you now: *Be of good cheer; I have overcome the world.* Because you belong to My kingdom, *in Me you may have Peace.*

JOHN 18:36; MATTHEW 26:53;
ACTS 2:21; JOHN 16:33 NKJV

I HAVE GOOD INTENTIONS FOR YOU. They may be radically different from what you hoped or expected, but they are nonetheless good. *I am Light; in Me there is no darkness at all.* So look for My Light in all your circumstances. I am abundantly present in your moments. Your assignment is to be open to Me and My ways with you. Sometimes this requires relinquishing things you had planned or dreamed. You need to remember and wholeheartedly believe that *My way is perfect*, no matter how hard it is.

I am a shield for all who take refuge in Me. When you're feeling afflicted or afraid, come to Me and say: "Lord, I take refuge in *You.*" I don't shield you from things I intend for you to deal with, for you have an important part to play in this world. However, I protect you from more dangers and troubles than you can imagine. So make every effort to *live the life I have assigned to you.* Do this in joyful dependence on Me, and *your soul will be richly satisfied.*

1 JOHN 1:5 NASB; PSALM 18:30;
1 CORINTHIANS 7:17 ESV; PSALM 63:5

SEEK TO BECOME increasingly receptive and responsive to Me. I am always actively involved in your life. Instead of trying to force Me to do what you want, *when* you want it, relax and look for what I'm already doing. Live in a receptive mode—waiting for Me, trusting in My timing. *I am good to those who wait hopefully and expectantly for Me.* Ask Me to open your eyes to see all that I have for you. Such awareness helps you live responsively, ready to do My will.

My followers often fail to see the many blessings I shower on them. They're so busy looking for other things that they miss what is before them—*or* is on the way. They forget I am sovereign God and the timing of events is My prerogative.

I want you to trust Me enough to let Me lead. When a couple is dancing, one of them leads and the other follows. Otherwise, there is confusion and awkwardness. Dance with *Me*, beloved. Follow My lead as I guide you gracefully through your life.

LAMENTATIONS 3:25 AMP;
EPHESIANS 5:17 NKJV;
PSALM 71:16; PSALM 28:7

I AM RICHLY PRESENT in the world around you, in the Word, and in your heart through My Spirit. Ask Me to open the eyes of your heart so that you can "see" Me—for I am lovingly present in all your moments. It's vital to set aside blocks of time for *seeking My Face*. This requires sustained mental discipline: pulling your thoughts back from the idols that entice you and choosing to think about Me. I am the living Word, so you will find Me vibrantly present when you search for Me in the Scriptures.

I created breathtaking beauty in the world, to point you to the One who made everything. *Without Me, nothing was made that has been made.* Whenever you are enjoying something beautiful, thank Me. This pleases Me, and it also increases your pleasure. When you encounter difficult, ugly things in this broken world, trust Me then too. Keep looking for Me in the midst of your good times *and* your hard times. Find hope and comfort through knowing that *all your times are in My hands.*

1 CHRONICLES 16:11;
JOHN 1:3; PSALM 31:14–15 NKJV

I AM THE LORD YOUR GOD, who takes hold of your right hand and says to you, Do not fear; I will help you. It is essential for you to recognize—and believe—that I am not only your Savior, I am also *your God.* Many people try to cast Me as a great human model, a martyr who sacrificed everything for others. But if I were only human, you would still be *dead in your sins.* The One who takes hold of your hand and calms your fears is the living God! Rejoice as you ponder this astonishing truth. Delight in the mysterious wonder of the Trinity—Father, Son, and Spirit—one God.

Take time to wait in My Presence. Tell Me your troubles; *pour out your heart before Me.* Hear Me saying, "Do not be afraid, beloved. I am here—ready to help you." I don't condemn you for your fears, but I do want you to displace them with hope and trust in Me. As you trustingly *put your hope in Me, My unfailing Love rests upon you.*

ISAIAH 41:13; EPHESIANS 2:1;
PSALM 62:8 NKJV; PSALM 33:22

BE STILL IN MY PRESENCE, and wait patiently for Me to act. Stillness is a rare commodity in this world. Many people judge themselves and their day by how much they have accomplished. Resting in My Presence is usually not one of those accomplishments. Yet how much blessing can be found in this holy rest!

Peace and Joy abound in My Presence, but it takes time for them to soak into your inner being. It also takes trust. Instead of fussing and fuming when your plans are thwarted, wait patiently for Me to act. You can *watch in hope for Me* because I am *God your Savior.* Be assured that *I will hear you.* I may not answer as soon as you would like, but I always respond to your prayers in the best way.

Don't worry about evil people or fret about their wicked schemes. I laugh at the wicked, for I know their day is coming. Rest in Me, beloved. *Be still, and know that I am God.*

PSALM 37:7 NLT; MICAH 7:7;
PSALM 37:13; PSALM 46:10 NKJV

YOU HAVE RECEIVED *NEW BIRTH* into a living *hope through My resurrection from the dead.* I died on the cross to pay the penalty for the sins of all My followers. However, if I had remained dead, *your faith would be useless* and you would forever be spiritually dead—*still guilty of your sins.* Of course, it was impossible for My death to be permanent because I am God! As I stated clearly to those who questioned Me, *I and My Father are One.*

My resurrection is an extremely well-documented historical fact. This miraculous event opened the way for you to experience *new birth.* By confessing your sinfulness and trusting Me as your Savior, you have become one of My own—walking along a pathway to heaven. Because I am your living Savior, you walk along a way of *living hope!* The Light of My loving Presence shines upon you always, even in your darkest, most difficult moments. Look up to Me, beloved. Let My brilliant Love-Light pierce the darkness and fill your heart with Joy.

1 PETER 1:3; 1 CORINTHIANS 15:17 NLT;
EPHESIANS 2:1; JOHN 10:30 NKJV

DO NOT BE AFRAID; *do not be discouraged.* You are looking ahead at uncertainties, letting them unnerve you. Fear and discouragement are waiting alongside your pathway into the future—ready to accompany you if you let them. *Yet I am always with you, holding you by your right hand.* Because I live beyond time, I am also on the path up ahead—shining brightly, beckoning you on, encouraging you to fix your gaze on Me. Cling tightly to My hand, and walk resolutely past those dark presences of fearfulness and despair. Keep looking toward My radiant Presence that beams out rays of *unfailing Love* and endless encouragement.

Your confidence comes from knowing I am continually with you *and* I am already in your future, preparing the way before you. Listen as I call back to you—words of warning and wisdom, courage and hope: *Do not fear, for I am with you. Do not be dismayed, for I am your God. I will strengthen you and help you; I will uphold you with My righteous right hand.*

DEUTERONOMY 31:8; PSALM 73:23;
PSALM 119:76; ISAIAH 41:10

BELOVED, *MY COMPASSIONS NEVER FAIL. They are new every morning.* So you can begin each day confidently, knowing that My vast reservoir of blessings is full to the brim. This knowledge helps you *wait for Me,* entrusting your long-unanswered prayers into My care and keeping. I assure you that not one of those petitions has slipped past Me unnoticed. I want you to drink deeply from My fountain of limitless Love and unfailing compassion. As you wait in My Presence, these divine nutrients are freely available to you.

Although many of your prayers are not yet answered, you can find hope in *My great faithfulness.* I keep all My promises in My perfect way and timing. I have promised to *give you Peace* that can displace the trouble and fear in your heart. If you become weary of waiting, remember that I also wait—*that I may be gracious to you and have mercy on you.* I hold back till you're ready to receive the things I have lovingly prepared for you. *Blessed are all those who wait for Me.*

LAMENTATIONS 3:22–24;
JOHN 14:27; ISAIAH 30:18 NKJV

NEVER UNDERESTIMATE the power of prayer! People who are feeling discouraged and hopeless often say something like, "There's nothing left to do but pray." The implication is that this is their last resort—and a feeble one at that. Nothing could be further from the truth!

I created mankind with the ability to communicate with Me. Since I am *the eternal, immortal, invisible King* of the universe, this is an astonishing privilege. Even when the human race became tainted with sin through Adam and Eve's disobedience, I did not withdraw this glorious privilege. And when I lived in your world as a flesh-and-blood man, I relied heavily on praying to My Father. I was keenly aware of how continuously I needed His help.

Persistent, heartfelt prayer will bless not only you but also your family, friends, church—even your country. Ask the Holy Spirit to help you pray effectively. Find others to join you in this venture of seeking My Face in humility and repentance. Beseech Me to *heal your land.*

COLOSSIANS 1:16 NKJV;
1 TIMOTHY 1:17; MATTHEW 14:23 NKJV;
2 CHRONICLES 7:14

WHEN YOU BUMP INTO massive difficulties on your life-path, I want you to *consider it pure Joy.* As you bounce off these "impossibilities," *My everlasting arms* are wide open—ready to catch you, calm you, and help you do what does not seem possible. You can be joyful in the midst of perplexing problems because I am *God your Savior*—and I have already accomplished the greatest miracle in your life: saving you from your sins. If you keep looking to Me, your resurrected Lord and King, your pessimism will eventually give way to courage. Though you are an earthbound creature, your soul shares in My eternal victory.

I have infinite Power, so "impossibilities" are My specialty. I delight in them because they display My Glory so vividly. They also help you live the way I intended: in joyful, trusting dependence on Me. The next time you face an "impossible" situation, turn to Me immediately with a hopeful heart. Acknowledge your total inadequacy and cling to Me—relying on My infinite sufficiency. *All things are possible with Me!*

JAMES 1:2–3; DEUTERONOMY 33:27 NKJV;
HABAKKUK 3:17–18; MATTHEW 19:26

FIND YOUR SECURITY IN ME. As the world you inhabit seems increasingly unsafe, turn your attention to Me more and more often. Remember that I am with you at *all* times, and I have already won the ultimate victory. Because *I am in you and you are in Me*, you have an eternity of perfect, stress-free life awaiting you. There will be no trace of fear or worry in heaven. Reverential worship of *the King of Glory* will flood you with unimaginable Joy!

Let this *future hope* strengthen and encourage you while you're living in this deeply fallen world. When you start to feel anxious about something you have seen, heard, or thought, bring that concern to Me. Remind yourself that *I* am the One who makes you secure—in all circumstances! If you find your mind gravitating toward an idolatrous way of feeling safe, tell yourself: "*That's* not what makes me safe." Then look trustingly to Me, and think about who I am: the victorious Savior-God who is your Friend forever. In Me you are absolutely secure!

JOHN 14:20; PSALM 24:7 NKJV;
PROVERBS 23:18

I GIVE STRENGTH TO THE WEARY and increase the power of the weak. So do not be discouraged by your weakness. There are many kinds of weaknesses, and no one is exempt from all of them. I use them to keep My loved ones humble and to train them to wait on Me in trusting dependence. I have promised that *those who wait on Me will gain new strength.*

This waiting is not meant to be practiced only *sometimes*. I designed you to look to Me continually, knowing Me as *the Living One who sees you* always. Waiting on Me is closely related to trusting Me. The more time you spend focusing on Me, the more you will trust Me. And the more you trust Me, the more you will want to spend time with Me. Waiting on Me in the midst of your moments also increases your hope in Me. This hope blesses you in countless ways— lifting you above your circumstances, enabling you to *praise Me for the help of My Presence.*

ISAIAH 40:29; ISAIAH 40:30–31 NASB;
GENESIS 16:14 AMP; PSALM 42:5 NASB

YOUR PRAYERS ARE NOT CRIES IN THE DARK; they rise to My kingdom of glorious Light. *Call to Me, and I will answer you and show you great and mighty things.* Mankind has long been plagued with eyes that do not see what is most important. People often fail to perceive the most obvious things. I can perform miracles before their very eyes, yet they see only mundane occurrences—or label them coincidences. Only *the eyes of your heart* can perceive spiritual realities.

I delight in people who have a *teachable* attitude. When you come to Me eager to learn *great things which you do not know,* I rejoice. A good teacher takes pleasure in a student who puts forth extra effort to discover new things. I am pleased with your desire to learn wondrous things from Me. Your openness to My teaching helps you understand *the hope to which I have called you, the riches of My glorious inheritance* in which you share. You can look forward to living with Me in the Holy City, where *the Glory of God provides Light.*

JEREMIAH 33:3 NKJV; EPHESIANS 1:18;
PSALM 143:10; REVELATION 21:23

I DELIGHT IN THOSE WHO FEAR ME, who put their hope in My unfailing Love. "Fear of the Lord" is often misunderstood, but it is the foundation of spiritual wisdom and knowledge. It consists of reverential awe, adoration, and submission to My will. You submit to Me by exchanging *your* attitudes and goals for *Mine.* Since I am your Creator, aligning yourself with Me is the best way to live. When your lifestyle exhibits this biblical fear, I take delight in you. Seek to feel My pleasure shining on you at such times.

Living according to My will is not easy; there will be many ups and downs as you journey with Me. But no matter what is happening, you can find hope in My unfailing Love. In your world today, many people are feeling desperate. They've become disillusioned and cynical because they put their confidence in the wrong thing. But *My steadfast Love* will never let you down—it will never let you go! Cling to hope, beloved. It's a golden cord connecting you to Me.

PSALM 147:11; PROVERBS 1:7 NKJV;
LAMENTATIONS 3:22–23 ESV

WHEN YOUR WORLD LOOKS DARK and threatening, come to Me. *Pour out your heart to Me*, knowing that I'm listening—and I care. Find comfort in My sovereignty: I'm in control even when global events look terribly out of control. Actually, many things are *not* as they should be, *not* as they were created to be. You do well to yearn for perfect goodness—someday those longings will be wondrously satisfied.

Consider the prophet Habakkuk as he awaited the Babylonian invasion of Judah. He knew the attack would be brutal, and he wrestled deeply with this prophetic knowledge. Finally, though, he wrote a hymn of absolute confidence in Me. After describing utterly desperate circumstances, he concluded: *"Yet I will rejoice in the LORD, I will be joyful in God my Savior."*

Feel free to wrestle with Me about your concerns. But remember that the goal is to come to a place of confident trust and transcendent Joy. You won't understand My mysterious ways, but you can find hope and help in My Presence. *I am your Strength!*

PSALM 62:8 NLT; REVELATION 22:5;
HABAKKUK 3:17–19; PSALM 42:5 NASB

LET MY UNFAILING LOVE be your comfort. "Comfort" eases grief and trouble; it also gives strength and hope. The best source of these blessings is My constant Love that will never, ever fail you. No matter what is happening in your life, this Love can console you and cheer you up. However, you must make the effort to turn to Me for help. I am always accessible to you, and I delight in giving you everything you need.

I have complete, perfect understanding of you and your circumstances. My grasp of your situation is far better than yours. So beware of being overly introspective—trying to figure things out by looking inward, leaving Me out of the equation. When you realize you have done this, turn to Me with a brief prayer: "Help me, Jesus." Remind yourself that *I* am the most important part of the equation of your life! Relax with Me awhile, letting My loving Presence comfort you. *In the world you will have trouble; but be of good cheer, I have overcome the world.*

PSALM 119:76; PSALM 29:11;
PSALM 42:5 NASB; JOHN 16:33 NKJV

LEARN TO BE JOYFUL when things don't go as you would like. Do not begin your day determined to make everything go your way. Each day you will bump up against at least one thing that doesn't yield to your will. It could be as trivial as the reflection you see in the mirror or as massive as a loved one's serious illness or injury. My purpose for you is *not* to grant your every wish or to make your life easy. My desire is that you learn to trust Me in all circumstances.

If you are intent upon having your way in everything, you will be frustrated much of the time. I don't want you to waste energy regretting things that have happened. The past cannot be changed, but you have My help in the present and My hope for the future. So try to relax—trusting in My control over your life. Remember: I am always close to you, and there is abundant *Joy in My Presence.* In fact, *My Face radiates with Joy* that shines upon you!

PSALM 62:8; PROVERBS 23:18;
ACTS 2:28; NUMBERS 6:25 TLB

THANKFULNESS IS THE BEST ANTIDOTE to a sense of entitlement—the poisonous attitude that "the world owes me." This misconception is epidemic in the work world, and it is contrary to biblical teaching. The apostle Paul commanded Christians to "keep away from every brother who is idle." Paul also taught by example—*working day and night to make himself a model for others to follow.* He even gave this rule: "If a man will not work, he shall not eat."

One definition of entitlement is *the feeling or belief that you deserve to be given something.* Thankfulness is the opposite: a grateful attitude for what you *already* have. If I gave you what you deserved, your ultimate destination would be hell—you would have no hope of salvation. So be thankful that I am *rich in mercy; it is by grace you have been saved.*

Thinking that you deserve more than you currently have will make you miserable, but a grateful attitude will fill you with Joy. Moreover, when you are thankful, you *worship Me acceptably with reverence and awe.*

2 THESSALONIANS 3:6–10; EPHESIANS 2:4–5;
PSALM 107:1 NKJV; HEBREWS 12:28

I, THE LORD, AM *YOUR STRENGTH*. On days when you are feeling strong, this truth may not speak powerfully to you. However, it is a lifeline full of encouragement and hope, and it is always available to you. Whenever you're feeling weak, your lack of strength can help you look to Me and cling to this secure lifeline. You may call out to Me at any time, *"Lord, save me!"*

Let *My unfailing Love be your comfort*. When you seem to be sinking in your struggles, it's crucial to hold onto something that will not fail you, something you can trust with your very life. My powerful Presence not only strengthens you; it holds you close and doesn't let go. I have a firm grip on you, beloved.

Because I am always near, there's no need to fear being weak. In fact, *My Strength comes into its own in your weakness*; the two fit together perfectly. So, thank Me for your weaknesses—trusting in My ever-present Strength.

PSALM 59:17; MATTHEW 14:30;
PSALM 119:76; 2 CORINTHIANS 12:9 MSG

THE PROSPECT OF THE RIGHTEOUS IS JOY.
This means your prospects are excellent, for I have
clothed you with My *robe of righteousness.* So begin
each day eager to receive the Joy I have in store for you.

Some of My followers fail to find the pleasures I
have prepared for them because they focus too much
on problems in their lives and trouble in the world.
Instead of living *to the full*, they live cautiously, seeking to minimize pain and risk. In doing so, they also
minimize their Joy and their effectiveness in My kingdom. This is *not* My way for you.

As you awaken each morning, seek My Face with
hopeful anticipation. Invite Me to prepare you not
only for any difficulties on the road ahead but also for
the pleasures I've planted alongside your path. Then
take My hand as you begin your journey through the
day, and let Me share in everything you encounter
along the way—including all the Joy!

PROVERBS 10:28;
ISAIAH 61:10 NKJV; JOHN 10:10

JOY IS A CHOICE—one that you face many times each day as long as you live in this world. When you graduate to heaven, indescribably glorious Joy will be yours—effortlessly. You won't have to exert your will to be joyful. It will come naturally and be constant.

While you journey through this fallen world, I want to help you make increasingly wise choices. You need to become aware—and stay aware—that you can choose to be positive and hopeful moment by moment. Make it your goal to find Joy in the midst of your day. If you notice that you're experiencing discouragement, frustration, or other negative feelings, let those prickly emotions prod you into remembering Me. *Seek My Face* and talk with Me. You can pray something like, "Jesus, I choose to be joyful because You are *God My Savior* and *nothing can separate me from Your loving Presence.*"

Live victoriously, beloved, by seeking to find Me in more and more of your moments.

PSALM 27:8 NKJV;
HABAKKUK 3:18; ROMANS 8:38–39

TO THE ONE WHO IS THIRSTY I will give water free of charge from the spring of the water of Life. Drink deeply from this spring so that I can live abundantly in you. Let the water of Life soak into the depths of your being, refreshing and renewing you. Since this Life-water is free, you can have as much of it as you want—as much of *Me* as you want. I am *Christ in you, the hope of Glory*!

I long for you to *thirst for Me, your God,* more and more. Thirst is a very powerful appetite; this is necessary because drinking sustains life even more than eating. Pure water is a much healthier choice than canned drinks full of sugar or chemicals. Similarly, thirsting for Me first and foremost is crucial for your spiritual health. Though other things may seem to satisfy you for a while, they will not slake the thirst of your soul.

Rejoice that what you need most is free of charge! *Joyously draw water from the springs of salvation.*

REVELATION 21:6 NET; COLOSSIANS 1:27;
PSALM 63:1 ESV; ISAIAH 12:3 NASB

EVEN THOUGH YOU DO NOT SEE ME, you believe in Me. I am far more real—complete, unchanging, unlimited—than the things you can see. When you believe in Me, you are trusting in rock-solid Reality. I am the indestructible *Rock* on which you can keep standing, no matter what your circumstances may be. And because you belong to Me, I am devoted to you. Beloved, I encourage you to *take refuge in Me.*

Believing in Me has innumerable benefits. The most precious one is *the salvation of your soul*— forever and ever. Your belief in Me also enhances your present life immensely, making it possible for you to know who you are and Whose you are. As you stay in communication with Me, I help you find your way through this fallen world with hope in your heart. All of this enlarges your capacity for Joy. The more you seek Me and the more fully you know Me, the more I can fill you with *inexpressible and glorious Joy!*

1 PETER 1:8–9; PSALM 18:2;
ROMANS 8:25 NKJV

AS YOU JOURNEY THROUGH LIFE with Me, see the hope of heaven shining on your path—lighting up your perspective. Remember that you are one of My *chosen people, belonging to Me. I called you out of darkness into My wonderful Light.* Savor the richness of these concepts: *I chose you before the creation of the world,* so nothing can separate you from Me. You belong to Me forever! I drew you out of the darkness *of sin and death* into the exquisite Light of eternal Life.

The brightness of My Presence helps you in multiple ways. The closer to Me you live, the more clearly you can see the way forward. As you soak in this Love-drenched Light, *I give you strength and bless you with Peace.* My radiance blesses not only you but also other people as it permeates your whole being. This time spent focusing on Me helps you become more like Me, enabling you to shine into the lives of others. I'm continually drawing My loved ones out of darkness into My glorious Light.

1 PETER 2:9; EPHESIANS 1:4;
ROMANS 8:2 ESV; PSALM 29:11 NKJV

No MATTER HOW LONELY you may feel, you are never alone. Christmas can be a hard time for people who are separated from loved ones. The separation may be a result of death, divorce, distance, or other causes. The holiday merriment around you can intensify your sense of aloneness. But all My children have a resource that is more than adequate to help them: My continual Presence.

Remember this prophecy about Me: *The virgin . . . will give birth to a Son, and they will call Him Immanuel—which means* "God with us." Long before I was born, I was proclaimed to be the God who is *with you*. This is rock-solid truth that nobody and no circumstance can take away from you.

Whenever you're feeling lonely, take time to enjoy My Presence. Thank Me for *wrapping you with a robe of righteousness* to make you righteous. Ask Me—*the God of hope*—to *fill you with Joy and Peace.* Then, through the help of My Spirit, you can *overflow with hope* into the lives of other people.

ISAIAH 7:14; ISAIAH 61:10 NASB;
2 CORINTHIANS 5:21 NKJV; ROMANS 15:13

I AM THE LIGHT OF THE WORLD! Many people celebrate Advent season by illuminating their homes with candles and decorated trees. This is a way of symbolizing My coming into the world—eternal Light breaking through the darkness and opening up the way to heaven. Nothing can reverse this glorious plan of salvation. All who trust Me as Savior are adopted into My royal family forever!

My Light shines on in the darkness, for the darkness has never overpowered it. No matter how much evil and unbelief you see in this dark world, I continue to shine brightly—a beacon of hope to those who have eyes that really see. So it's crucial to look toward the Light as much as possible. *Fix your eyes on Me,* beloved! Through thousands of good thought-choices, you can find Me—"see" Me—as you journey through this life. My Spirit can help you persevere in the delightful discipline of keeping your eyes on Me. *Whoever follows Me will never walk in darkness but will have the Light of Life.*

JOHN 8:12; EPHESIANS 1:5 NLT;
JOHN 1:5 AMP; HEBREWS 12:2

THE CHRISTIAN LIFE is all about trusting Me: in good times *and* in hard times. I am Lord over all your circumstances, so I want to be involved in every aspect of your life. You can quickly connect with Me by affirming your confidence in Me here and now. When your world seems dark and you trust Me anyway, My Light shines brightly through you. Your display of transcendent faith weakens spiritual forces of evil. And My supernatural Light showing through you blesses and strengthens people around you.

Clinging to Me in the dark requires you to persistently exert your willpower. But while you're grasping onto Me, remember: My hand has an eternal grip on yours—I will never let go of you! Moreover, My Spirit helps you keep hanging on. When you feel on the verge of giving up, cry out for His assistance: "Help me, Holy Spirit!" This brief prayer enables you to tap into His limitless resources. Even when your circumstances look dark and threatening, My Light is still *shining on* in surpassing splendor!

1 JOHN 1:7; PSALM 62:8;
PSALM 139:10 NKJV; JOHN 1:5 AMP

RELAX, MY CHILD. I'm in control. Let these words wash over you repeatedly, like soothing waves on a beautiful beach, assuring you of My endless Love. You waste a lot of time and energy trying to figure out things before their time has come. Meanwhile, I am working to prepare the way before you. So be on the lookout for some wonderful surprises—circumstances that only *I* could have orchestrated.

Remember that you are My beloved. I am on your side, and I want what is best for you. Someone who is loved by a generous, powerful person can expect to receive an abundance of blessings. *You* are loved by the King of the universe, and I have good plans for you. As you look ahead into the unknown future, relax in the knowledge of who you are—*the one I love.* Cling to My hand, and go forward with confidence. While you and I walk together along *the path of Life,* your trust in Me will fill your heart with Joy and your mind with Peace.

JEREMIAH 29:11; DEUTERONOMY 33:12;
PSALM 16:11 NKJV

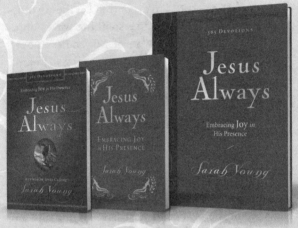

If you liked reading this book,
you may enjoy these other titles by

Sarah Young

Jesus Calling
Enjoying Peace in His Presence
ISBN 9781591451884

Jesus Today
Experience Hope Through His Presence
ISBN 9781400320097

Jesus Lives
Seeing His Love in Your Life
ISBN 9781400320943

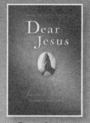

Dear Jesus
Seeking His Light in Your Life
ISBN 9781404104952

Learn more at JesusCalling.com